EDITED BY **WADE HUDSON & CHERYL WILLIS HUDSON**

# THE TALK

## CONVERSATIONS ABOUT
## RACE, LOVE & TRUTH

CROWN BOOKS FOR YOUNG READERS
NEW YORK

"Remember This" copyright © 2020 by Renée Watson, illustration copyright © 2020 by Shadra Strickland. "Handle Your Business" copyright © 2020 by Derrick Barnes, illustration copyright © 2020 by Gordon C. James. "Not a China Doll" text and illustration copyright © 2020 by Grace Lin. "The Bike" copyright © 2020 by Wade Hudson, illustration copyright © 2020 by E. B. Lewis. "The Way of the Anigiduwagi" copyright © 2020 by Traci Sorell, illustration copyright © 2020 by MaryBeth Timothy. Untitled copyright © 2020 by Daniel Nayeri, illustration copyright © 2020 by Zeke Peña. "Why Are There Racist People?" text and illustration copyright © 2020 by Duncan Tonatiuh. "Never Be Afraid to Soar" copyright © 2020 by Valerie Wilson Wesley, illustration copyright © 2020 by Don Tate. "My Olmec" text and illustration copyright © 2020 by Selina Alko. "F.R.I.E.N.D.S." copyright © 2020 by Torrey Maldonado, illustration copyright © 2020 by Natacha Bustos. "TEN" copyright © 2020 by Tracey Baptiste, illustration copyright © 2020 by April Harrison. "I'm a Dancer" copyright © 2020 by Sharon Dennis Wyeth, illustration copyright © 2020 by Raul Colón. "Hablar" copyright © 2020 by Meg Medina, illustration copyright © 2020 by Rudy Gutierrez. "Our Inheritance" copyright © 2020 by Adam Gidwitz, illustration copyright © 2020 by Peter H. Reynolds. "Tough Tuesday" copyright © 2020 by Nikki Grimes, illustration copyright © 2020 by Erin K. Robinson. "The Road Ahead" copyright © 2020 by Minh Lê, illustration copyright © 2020 by Cozbi A. Cabrera. "Mazes" text and illustration copyright © 2020 by Christopher Myers.

All rights reserved. Published in the United States by Crown Books for Young Readers, an imprint of Random House Children's Books, a division of Penguin Random House LLC, New York.

Crown and the colophon are registered trademarks of Penguin Random House LLC.

Visit us on the Web! rhcbooks.com

Educators and librarians, for a variety of teaching tools,
visit us at RHTeachersLibrarians.com

Library of Congress Cataloging-in-Publication Data
Names: Hudson, Wade, editor. | Hudson, Cheryl Willis, editor.
Title: The talk: conversations about race, love & truth / edited by Wade Hudson & Cheryl Willis Hudson
Other titles: The talk, conversations about race, love and truth
Description: New York: Crown Books for Young Readers, [2020] | Includes bibliographical references. | Summary: "Thirty diverse and award-winning authors and illustrators capture frank discussions about racism, identity, and self-esteem"—Provided by publisher.
Identifiers: LCCN 2020011095 (print) | LCCN 2020011096 (ebook) | ISBN 978-0-593-12161-0 (hardcover) | ISBN 978-0-593-12162-7 (library binding) | ISBN 978-0-593-12164-1 (trade paperback) | ISBN 978-0-593-12163-4 (ebook)
Subjects: LCSH: Racism—Juvenile literature. | Race relations—Juvenile literature. | African American children—Juvenile literature. | African Americans—Social conditions—Juvenile literature. | Minorities—United States—Juvenile literature. | Ethnic identity—Juvenile literature. | Self-esteem in children—Juvenile literature. | Conduct of life—Juvenile literature. | Encouragement—Juvenile literature. | Didactic literature, American.
Classification: LCC E185.61 .T19 2020 (print) | LCC E185.61 (ebook) | DDC 305.800973—dc23

The text of this book is set in 12.5-point Neutraface 2 Text.
Interior design by Monique Razzouk

Printed in the United States of America
10 9 8 7 6 5 4 3 2 1
First Edition

Random House Children's Books supports the First Amendment and celebrates the right to read.

# FOR THOSE WHO ARE
# COURAGEOUS ENOUGH TO TALK

—W.H. & C.W.H.

# CONTENTS

**Foreword**
    by Wade Hudson and Cheryl Willis Hudson .......... VII

**"Remember This"**
    by Renée Watson, illustrated by Shadra Strickland .... 1

**"Handle Your Business"**
    by Derrick Barnes, illustrated by Gordon C. James .... 7

**"Not a China Doll"**
    by Grace Lin ......................................... 15

**"The Bike"**
    by Wade Hudson, illustrated by E. B. Lewis ........... 21

**"The Way of the Anigiduwagi"**
    by Traci Sorell, illustrated by MaryBeth Timothy ...... 27

**Untitled**
    by Daniel Nayeri, illustrated by Zeke Peña ............ 33

**"Why Are There Racist People?"**
    by Duncan Tonatiuh ................................. 39

**"Never Be Afraid to Soar"**
    by Valerie Wilson Wesley, illustrated by Don Tate ..... 49

**"My Olmec"**
    by Selina Alko ....................................... 55

**"F.R.I.E.N.D.S.: Looking Back, Looking Forward"**
    by Torrey Maldonado, illustrated by Natacha Bustos ... 63

**"TEN"**
by Tracey Baptiste, illustrated by April Harrison . . . . . . . 71

**"I'm a Dancer"**
by Sharon Dennis Wyeth, illustrated by Raul Colón . . . . 79

**"Hablar"**
by Meg Medina, illustrated by Rudy Gutierrez . . . . . . . . 87

**"Our Inheritance"**
by Adam Gidwitz, illustrated by Peter H. Reynolds . . . . 93

**"Tough Tuesday"**
by Nikki Grimes, illustrated by Erin K. Robinson . . . . . . . 103

**"The Road Ahead"**
by Minh Lê, illustrated by Cozbi A. Cabrera . . . . . . . . . . 107

**"Mazes"**
by Christopher Myers . . . . . . . . . . . . . . . . . . . . . . . . . . . . . . 113

**Sources and Notes from the Authors** . . . . . . . . . . . . . . . . . . . 125

**About the Authors and Artists** . . . . . . . . . . . . . . . . . . . . . . . 133

**Photo Credits** . . . . . . . . . . . . . . . . . . . . . . . . . . . . . . . . . . . . 148

# FOREWORD

There are many reasons why parents and caregivers share "The Talk" with children. For some, it's to prepare their daughter for the challenges she will surely face because she is female. Others have "The Talk" because of their youngster's sexual orientation. Immigrant parents have few options *but* to have it. And many have it because their child chooses to pursue an occupation, join a team, or participate in an organization where they were not often welcome because of their physical appearance.

The list goes on. There are myriad versions of "The Talk" because there are myriad ways to be *human*. And we wish we had the space to capture all of these conversations within these pages, because we know they are happening and we know people are hurting. This collection focuses on race, but we hope our readers see the words and images shared here as a starting point and a way we can all begin to build a more accepting world for each other.

In our home, we had "The Talk" with our daughter, Katura, and our son, Stephan. Many times. As adults responsible for two beautiful Black children, we knew how essential it was to give them the tools to make their way as safely as possible in a society that is too often hostile to them simply because they are African American. Especially as sometimes that hostility leads to the loss of Black life. So we drummed into them the dos and don'ts, the places to go and places to avoid, what to say, what *not* to say, and even how to say it. Just as our parents did for us. We desperately wanted to keep our kids protected, but we also didn't want to erode their positive self-esteem or sense of place in the world. Our talks were balancing acts indeed.

We can only imagine the kinds of talks that occur in homes and schools today because so many of us are being picked on, pushed aside, told we don't belong, or told to go back to where we came from. But we knew a group of people who would have that knowledge firsthand.

The outstanding writers and artists whose work is featured in this anthology are intimately familiar with these crucial discussions and know just how important they can be. "The Talk," as much as any conversation can, helped them become more aware and better equipped when faced with the challenges the world threw at them—challenges that their parents and loved ones anticipated. They share their experiences and the impact "The Talk" has had on their lives as well as the lessons they have passed on to their own children.

In these pages, the authors and illustrators use different forms and styles. There are letters, lists, poems, short stories, and essays. Illustrations are rendered in watercolor, collage, pen and ink, acrylic, comix frames, and digital styles. And their messages are as diverse as their mediums.

These revealing and frank moments expose lessons of empowerment and periods of shame, times when the contributors were told they were small and instances when role models insisted they were born to be *big*. With advice and love, harsh realities and encouraging words, the talks offered in this anthology are real conversations that embrace honest ways of thinking that help expand ourselves and others in a complex and diverse society. Too frequently, we are silenced from having tough conversations because we feel we don't have the words. But what these award-winning creators of books for children and young adults share in this collection are stories and images that are filled with love, acceptance, truth, peace, and an assurance that there can be hope for a better tomorrow and a better future for all of us. So, let's talk.

Wade Hudson
Cheryl Willis Hudson

LOVE RECOGNIZES
JUMPS HURDLES,
PENETRATES WALLS
DESTINATION FULL

NO BARRIERS. IT
LEAPS FENCES,
TO ARRIVE AT ITS
OF HOPE.

—MAYA ANGELOU

# REMEMBER THIS

by Renée Watson

illustrated by Shadra Strickland

And when the weight of being a Black girl feels like a burden and not a blessing, remember this.

Black girl, you are miracle. Know that you can survive what feels impossible to survive because someone somewhere prayed for you, is praying for you. Because someone somewhere already survived, is surviving.

Remember Lucille Clifton and Maya Angelou. Remember Fannie Lou Hamer and Shirley Chisholm. They will teach you how to love the kink of your hair, the width of your hips, the brown of your skin.

They will teach you how to heal and be whole, how to find beauty in brokenness.

They will teach you how to carry revolution in your bones.

Remember you have never been alone. You have always had a map, always had your ancestors showing you the way.

And if someone ever tries to silence you, speak for you and change your story, try to make you only one thing when you are so much more, remember you have your own voice.

Your voice is a weapon, always. Learn the power of its silence, the impact of its loudness. Remember there are many ways to speak. You don't always need words, but you do need courage.

So remember to be courageous. Remember you will only know how brave you are if you do the thing you are afraid of.

It is okay to be afraid.

It is okay to have emotions, Black girl.

It is okay to be angry, to be sad. Do not deny yourself the freedom to feel. Find a place for your fear and anger and sadness. It will be too much to hold. Release that heaviness in a poem, a song, a dance, a sketchbook, a journal. Take a walk, talk to a friend. Do not hold it in.

And when laughter comes—when you are feeling hope and love and peace—hold on tight. Remember to keep what comforts you close: a good book, a good song, a good friend, a good memory. You will need these when darkness comes.

And this is the thing that is hard to say, hard to know.

Darkness will come, may never stop coming. You will be free and not free all at once. Happy and also sorrowful.

Someone who ought to love you will not love you.

Someone who ought to protect you will not protect you.

Sometimes people can't be what you need them to be even when they want to.

But remember this.

It is never about them. It is always about you—your growth, your purpose, your integrity.

Remember this.

You do not have to prove anything.

All you have to do is be your best.

All you have to do is remember where you come from, whose legacy you've inherited.

Learn yourself, Black girl.

And when they try to make you forget, when they attempt to erase your history, remind them that you know.

And keep on knowing and remembering.

And keep on and on.

Keep on getting up after failure, after success, after darkness.

Get up always and remember that every morning you rise is a form of resistance, a protest, a beginning, a way to start over, a way to continue.

# HANDLE YOUR BUSINESS

by Derrick Barnes

illustrated by Gordon C. James

I was helping my son with his math homework at the dining room table. It was equivalent fraction models or something like that. But because he was eight years old going on thirty, his thoughts were all over the place. Out of the blue, in between math problems, he blurted out, "Daddy . . . yesterday in class, we read a book about a bunch of monkeys bouncing on a bed."

"Say what? Monkeys?" I replied.

"Yes, monkeys. And you know what else, Daddy? The teacher even said that we're going to do a play about it."

Out of all the magnificently written and illustrated books that have been recently created to highlight the joy and brilliance of Black boys and girls, the teacher decided that this third-grade classroom needed to learn about monkeys jumping on a bed?

I don't think so.

"And, Daddy, guess what else?" he continued. "A boy in my class, who I thought was a friend but may not be my friend after all, said to me, 'Aren't you happy that there's finally a book about some characters that look like you?'"

"CHARACTERS THAT LOOK LIKE YOU?!" Yeah, I couldn't believe it, either.

"So what did you tell him?" I asked. I knew that he wouldn't just let that slide. That's not his style.

"Well, that book is about monkeys, and I know I'm not a monkey. I told that boy that I'm a prince!" my son proudly proclaimed as he slammed one of his little fists down on the table. (That's my boy!)

"So then what did you say, li'l man? What did you tell him then?"

"I thought that maybe he was trying to be funny or something. 'Cause I know I didn't come from animals. I told him that my people come from a long line of geniuses, architects, scientists, lawyers, generals, chiefs, professors, writers, artists, ROYALTY!"

"Did the rest of the class hear you?" I asked.

"I made sure that they all heard me, Daddy. The teacher was listening, too."

"So did you break down the history to them?" I asked.

"Well . . . I told him that no matter where you come from, what color you are, what country or continent your people are from, we ALLLLL came from Africa. The first people on this planet were Black Africans!" he said with his little chest stuck out. "They looked like me, and they had kingdoms, and ran universities. They were the first to do things with medicine, created mathematics and everything, while the rest of the world lived in darkness. In caves. That's what I told him, Daddy."

"You broke it down to him like that, son?" I was just egging him on at that point. I love it when he gets on a roll.

He nodded and said, "You know it, Daddy. You know it." And just like that, he quickly turned his attention back to his math problem, jotting down equations, number lines, and the faces of his favorite anime characters.

While he was being creative, productive, and not so productive all at once, I thought about everything I'd like to give him, so that he'll be prepared to go out into this great big, beautiful, sometimes mess of a world. I am certain that he'll be a difference maker, and leave his own mark. Maybe he'll travel the world, fall in love, and have his own family. And maybe . . . or most certainly, he'll be confronted with prejudgment, and low-level stereotypes placed upon him based on nothing but blind ignorance and fear. And who wants to talk to their eight-and-a-half-year-old son about that kind of future? But it's imperative. If I don't, he may not know how to conduct himself in the company of strangers, of people who won't see him as a star, people who may not know his worth, how invaluable he is to me, to his mother, family, and our community. He means more than the world to me. He is my everything.

It burns my soul, singes the edges of my heart when I think of having to find a way to tell him that there will be places he will go, and people he will be confronted with, that when they see his bright brown eyes, his beaming smile and perfect Brown skin, they will see absolutely—nothing. That is the definition of heartbreaking. But that is also our reality in this land.

In this day and age.

So while he is still beneath my wing, while I am still molding an amazing human being, I will fill him with an overwhelming amount of love, guidance, confidence, support, and discipline. That's it. That's a daddy thing. What's also a daddy thing is going up to that school in the a.m. and making them scrap that entire disrespectful presentation that they planned.

So my li'l man squiggles a few patterns, digits, and designs, and then puts the finishing touches on a character that's a cross between a tiger and a dragon. Then he just jumps back into the conversation like he never left.

"And another thing, Daddy, I told him he better respect that and respect me. I mean, how are we going to understand each other if he doesn't know his history, my history, our history . . . the truth? I set him straight, Daddy."

"I know you did, son." I chuckled a bit, but not too much. I wanted him to know that I had nothing but mad respect for the way he handled his business.

And just like that, *ZAP,* his brain flipped back to math. "Boom! I got it, Daddy. It'll take six shaded areas to equal the rhombus on the right. I got it!"

Yes, you do, li'l man. Yes, you do.

# NOT A
# CHINA DOLL

by Grace Lin

To my daughter when she turns ten,

Right now you are five years old, and you love lots of cute things. We both do.

Cute baby ducklings!

Cute smiley cookies!

Cute bunny stickers!

So I know it might be confusing that I bristled when you were called a cute China doll.

Aren't you just a cute little China doll!

me, not happy

When people call you a China doll, it's not a nice thing - even if they think it is.

That is because for over 100 years here in the United States, people expected East Asian women - women who look like us - to be a certain way. For a long time, stories in books and movies created a false idea about women who look like us. They showed Asian women acting meek and powerless, and that impression only grew stronger because of the popular Chinese dolls sold in the stores.

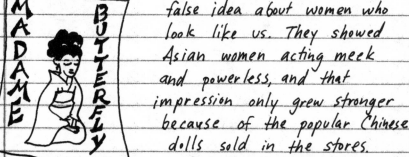

← an old story about a Japanese woman who falls in love with an American man (It has a tragic ending.)

Dolls only move the way you want them to move or say what you want them to say. Dolls only do what you want. Dolls are powerless.

So when people admire you because you are "a cute China doll," they are saying that they like you because you remind them of a toy. They might not

China doll

mean it in an unkind way, but it diminishes you. It makes you smaller. That is why when I said, "Thank you, but she's a girl, not a doll," I made sure you heard it.

Now that you are older, some boys might call you a China doll, too. And they also will probably mean it as a compliment. But I want you to know that it is _not_ a compliment.

Because if a boy is calling you a China doll or something like that, he is imagining that he can control you. He might not realize it, but he is imagining that you will do what he wants — that you will act and think the way he wants you to. He is imagining that you are a toy.

But you are _not_ a toy. You are a person. You have thoughts. You are in control of yourself and your body. You can say whatever you wish. You can do what you want. You are so much more than an object, a toy, or a doll.

You, a real person

You are a beautiful, imperfect human being who feels and thinks and acts with your own power.

You are _not_ a China doll.

Love,

your mother

_signature_

# THE BIKE

by Wade Hudson

illustrated by E. B. Lewis

## SCHWINN JAGUAR. THREE-SPEED GEARS, HAND BRAKES FOR LIVELY PERFORMANCE, BALLOON TIRES FOR SMOOTH RIDING

The bicycle ad in the newspaper seemed to leap off the page as I looked at it, beaming.

"Just what I want for Christmas," I told my brother PG, showing him the ad.

"I want one, too," he seconded.

If you were growing up in Mansfield, Louisiana, when I was a kid, you had to have a bike.

PG and I ran to the living room to show our parents the ad.

"Dad! Mom!" I yelled. "This is what I want for Christmas." I held the ad out for my father to see.

"It's a Schwinn. The newest model."

"I want one, too!" PG chimed in.

My father looked at the ad from a distance as if he didn't want to see it. Mom didn't look at it at all.

"Don't bother your father," she said, continuing to mend a torn shirt of mine. "He's trying to rest. Christmas is still a ways off."

My father finally spoke. "We'll see, son, we'll see" is all he said.

I was eight, and PG was seven. I couldn't wait to get my very own bicycle. We had learned to ride our neighbor's bike. But there was nothing like having your own.

PG and I were so excited as we lay in our bed on Christmas Eve. We could barely fall asleep. We just knew we would have our bikes the next morning. Our Christmas tree would be small, too small to place the bikes under it. So we knew when we arose early on Christmas morning, in the middle of our living room floor, there would be two Schwinn bicycles.

I awoke first and began rubbing the sleep from my eyes. I looked over at PG, who was still sleeping.

"PG! PG! It's morning!" I said, shaking my brother to wake him. "Let's go see our bikes!"

We both jumped out of bed and ran as fast as we could to the living room. But there were no bicycles.

"We didn't get 'em," PG said in a dejected voice.

Tears began to well up in my eyes. Softly, I said to PG, "No, I guess we didn't."

However, there on the sofa were two gun-and-holster sets just like the ones cowboy stars on television donned.

"We got a cap gun and holster last Christmas!" I complained in a raised voice.

I walked slowly back to our bedroom, got into bed, and pulled the covers over my head. It wasn't Christmas to me.

While everyone was up and about, enjoying Christmas, I remained in bed.

"Son?" I heard a voice call.

It was my father, who had walked quietly into the room.

"I know you wanted a bicycle for Christmas," he said as he approached the bed. "If it was at all possible, we would have gotten one for you. And your brother, too."

I had never seen such a pained look on my father's face before.

He continued. "We just couldn't afford it. There are five other children we have to buy gifts for. On top of that, we have a lot of bills to pay . . . a *lot* of bills! We don't like to worry y'all, but sometimes we have it tough. But we hang in there and try to do the best we can for all of you."

Then my father sat on the bed and looked me right in the eyes.

"Don't you know," he said, "if your mom and me could afford to get a bike for you, we would do it in a heartbeat?"

He rose and started what seemed like a long walk to the door, then stopped and turned to face me again.

"It won't always be this way! We won't always be poor and struggling." Then he left the room.

I remained in bed for a while, thinking about what my father had said. His words had touched me, reached me. That was the first time I had ever heard him use the words "poor" or "struggling."

My dad and mom always did all they could for us. We had a happy family life, enjoyed each other, loved each other, believed in each other. Not having enough money couldn't stop that. And not getting a bicycle for Christmas shouldn't stop that, either.

Suddenly, I realized PG and I hadn't gotten gifts for our parents. I jumped out of bed and ran to PG.

"We didn't get gifts for Mom and Dad," I told him. "The store down the street is still open. Let's go see what we can find. I got some change."

I pushed my right hand into the pocket of my jeans and pulled out a few quarters, dimes, and nickels.

"You're not mad about the bikes?" PG asked pointedly.

"Not anymore. If Dad and Mom could have afforded to get them, they would have."

PG nodded.

We ran as fast as we could to the corner store. There we found gifts. A set of handkerchiefs for each. Once we got home, we found old wrapping paper and wrapped them as neatly as we could. Mom gave us a big hug when we handed the gift to her. Dad held his gift for a looooong time, just staring at it. Finally, he looked at me, then at PG.

"You know, this is the best Christmas present I have ever received," he said. "This is a special Christmas."

# THE WAY OF THE ANIGIDUWAGI

by Traci Sorell

illustrated by MaryBeth Timothy

I want many things for you in this life, but most importantly, I pray for your ability to walk with honor and a solid cultural identity in every season of your life. That will be a challenge, as many circumstances and some people will not desire for either of those to have a firm hold on you. But there are other things you need to know that are already becoming part of your daily existence and awareness as a Cherokee young person and, very soon, asan adult.

Some will envy your lineage. Many will claim to be Cherokee when they are not. They want to be indigenous to this land. But only those from Native Nations living here since time immemorial have that legal identity as dual citizens of their tribes and of the United States. You come from strong people who have survived repeated attempts to be assimilated or annihilated. That is why it's important to learn our language, be involved in ceremonial life, and carry out your responsibilities as a Cherokee citizen.

Measures of success in the mainstream culture of the United States do not mirror ours. You will see some of our people, including those in leadership positions, lose themselves and our way of life in pursuit of that success.

Achievements in school or at work are never more important than caring about other living creatures.

Everyone has a role in a family, in a clan, in a community, and in a nation. You know this. You are being raised with a Cherokee worldview that recognizes that we are responsible for the well-being of those around us and the world in which we live. As you listen to others, you'll find that some are continually degraded through language, stereotypes, jokes, and attitudes that portray them as lesser, worthy of being victimized, and not seen as the sacred beings you have been raised to know them to be. Those words lead to harmful actions. Call out anyone suggesting or acting otherwise. We all carry this daily responsibility.

Also, folks will say and do some pretty demeaning things while telling you that they are "honoring" Native people. Don't buy it for a minute. We're not mascots, products to be sold, or a spiritual belief system to be appropriated. All of this causes real damage through lower self-worth, abuse, violence, and trafficking of our people. It also results in adults who enact policies that harm our continued existence and that of elohi, the world that provides everything we need to survive.

Though your culture may be invisible in mainstream society, you are enough. Your ancestors endured many hardships, and yet you are here. That ability to survive, adapt, and thrive despite horrific circumstances is in your DNA, along with the capacity to love deeply, serve generously, and shape your legacy by acting with integrity and gratitude in all you do. That is the way of the anigidu-wagi, they who are covered or rise above, as we call ourselves in our language. And that is who you are.

### PRONUNCIATION GUIDE:
- anigiduwagi: ah-NEE-gee-doo-hwah-gee
- elohi: eh-LOW-hee

by Daniel Nayeri

illustrated by Zeke Peña

Don't talk too much.
Persian poems don't have titles, but you're
  in the middle so I gave this one the title
  "Talking About Talking."

Don't walk into any rooms you can't walk
  out of.
Don't be proud of anything you don't know.
Don't go around throwing soft jabs.
  Pick your targets, and step through your
  punches.

All fighting is for blood.
All authority is backed by violence.
All the wishing in the world isn't worth
  a day of practice.

Fear is fine, but panic is weakness.
Fear lazy minds.
If you're strong and calm and wakeful, they'll
  fear you, even if you smile.

They is you and everyone you'll ever meet.
They is the talking gaggle of Babel.
They is the kids who sit at the table and wait
    to be fed.

You are my only son, and you eat what
    you kill.
You win or you learn.
You are the most fearsome creature in any
    forest or alley or country club.

Your job is to carry more than
    everyone you love.
Your shoulders are broad and will be your
    children's rightful throne.
Your mind is the fanciest thing
    you've got.

If they come for you, breathe deep and
    control yourself.
If they batter you with questions,
    don't talk too much.
If you're unwelcome, be undeniable.

They won't remember what you said, only
    how you made them feel.
They feel afraid of God but have
    99 gods.

They is you and everyone you know.

That's it. There's more to say, but only face
   to face.

Don't collect anything but wisdom.
Don't talk too much.
Don't ever stop saying I love you.


*This is a poem I wrote as a letter to my son, about how
to conduct yourself, as both a young man and an out-
sider. As his father, my only goal for him is that he gains
the strength to do good and the wisdom to know what
good is. That is the purpose of a man, as I express it to
him. And insofar as he accepts it, I tell him that you can
spot those men by how little nonsense comes out of their
mouths. We know this already, in the company of men,
and hear it expressed a thousand ways.*

*The great boxer Lennox Lewis described himself as
"silent, but violent." No chatter. Only the force of deter-
mination to impose his will on the world. Bruce Lee also
warned his students that "showing off is the fool's idea
of glory." And of course, the Bible says it most succinctly:
"Be slow to speak and slow to anger." That's about as
good a piece of advice as I could think of for a young man*

trying to engage with a world that is often unwelcoming, gossipy, and passive-aggressive.

As a young refugee to the United States, I spent a lot of time watching and listening as I tried to learn English. My own father stayed in Iran, and so I spoke to him only once a month, by phone. His advice was a lot like this poem. Short declarative sayings or aphorisms from Persian poetry. His advice was confusing most of the time. It would take him ten minutes just to explain the intricacies of one line of poetry. And after all that, it usually didn't have anything to do with my troubles as a third grader in Oklahoma. But over the years, I started to understand some of it. I started to see the lines of poetry as perfect crystallizations of common thoughts. And in my daily life, I would often see people who were covering for their lack of understanding by using more words.

I hope that the poem expresses some of this . . . that the most powerful person in any room is the one with the clearest thoughts and the fewest words.

# WHY ARE THERE RACIST PEOPLE?

by Duncan Tonatiuh

"Like, where does racism come from?" a student asked me while I was giving an author-illustrator presentation at his elementary school. I was not sure how to answer. I felt at a loss.

I know racism exists, and that it has existed in the past. It is a major theme of *Separate Is Never Equal,* one of the books I was sharing with students that day. The book is about how the Mendez family and other Latinx families in California in the 1940s joined together, filed a lawsuit, and fought to desegregate schools. At that time, children of Latinx origin in parts of California, Texas, Arizona, and New Mexico were sent to separate "Mexican" schools and were not allowed to go to class with white children.

In the book, I try to show how racism affected Latinx families and how courageous people stood up against it. But even though I have thought about how prejudice hurts people, I had never stopped to think deeply about where racism comes from.

I don't believe people are born racist. It is something they learn from others. But where did those other people learn it? What are the roots of racism? The question baffled me for months.

I looked for answers in books, articles, and documentaries. At some point, while reading about the history of the United States, I found a convincing explanation. At different times throughout history, selfish men have created unjust, racist laws and have spread racist attitudes as a way to divide the people they take advantage of. Prejudice has been used as a tool for these greedy men to protect their money and interests.

Let me give you an example. During the 1700s, most of the land and wealth in each American colony was owned by a few men who lived as if they were kings, while thousands lived under terrible conditions. In Boston in 1770, the top 1 percent of property owners owned 44 percent of the wealth. As one man put it, "Forty thousand would toil so that forty men could become rich."

Most of these men became wealthy by exploiting others. The land they owned was taken from Native Americans who were massacred or forced to flee. The fortunes they made often came from growing and selling crops. But they were not the ones working in the fields. The people working in the fields were Africans who had been forced to come to America and toiled from sunup to sundown as slaves. Or they were poor whites who had no land of their own and had to work for miserable wages or as indentured servants.

The rich landowners feared attacks from Native Americans. They were also scared of slave revolts and uprisings from the poor. But the wealthy had guns, and they had money to pay other men to protect them. What the rich feared the most, though, was that the different groups of people they abused would join together and stand up against them. If Native Americans, African Americans, and poor whites joined forces, they would be an army of thousands against a few hundred at most.

At that time only landowners could vote. The wealthy took advantage of this and created laws to prevent oppressed groups from joining together. They made it a crime for whites to marry or have children with blacks. They made it illegal for whites and blacks to go into Native American territories. The ruling landowners fostered fear and animosity.

A similar pattern can be seen at other times in U.S. history. I believe something comparable is happening today. There is an enormous amount of wealth in America, but like in colonial times, there is also tremendous inequality. Most of the country's money is concentrated in the hands of a small group of people, while millions of Americans have to work two or three jobs in order to pay for basic needs like housing, food, and transportation. Recent studies show that the 400 richest Americans have more wealth than 150 million people—almost half the population of the United States.

Research indicates that this inequality will continue to grow. The current system favors the super rich so they can become even wealthier, while millions of working Americans suffer.

We should be outraged by this. We should be protesting. But I think one of the reasons we aren't protesting is

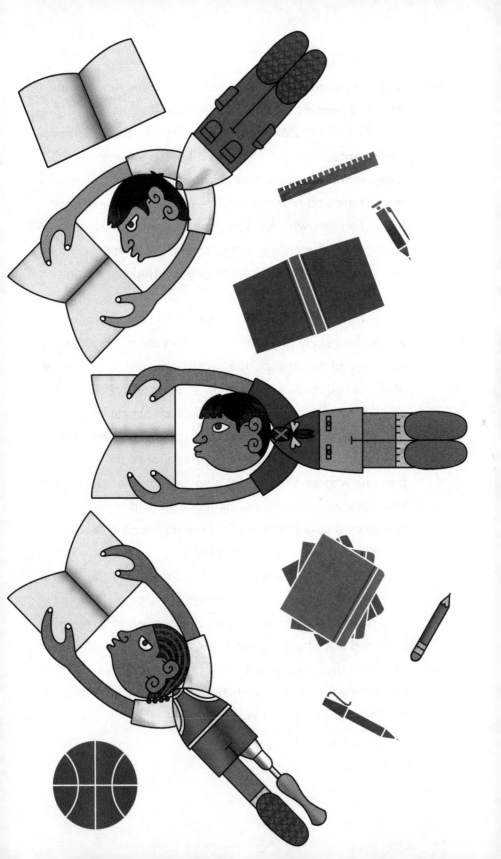

that politicians and other people in power have created laws and policies to divide us and distract us.

After the 2016 election, policies against Muslims, immigrants, and other minorities have been passed. Government leaders and commentators in the media foster hate and fear, especially among the growing numbers of whites who are struggling financially. They want to convince them that immigrants are stealing their jobs and that people of color are making their communities unsafe.

If working Americans are pitted against one another, we are less likely to join together. Instead of being angry and fearful toward people who look different, speak other languages, or practice a different religion, we should recognize that most of us face similar economic and social challenges. We should be upset at the greedy owners and shareholders of large corporations who don't pay fair wages. We should also be upset at politicians who receive large donations from the super rich and in turn create laws that benefit them disproportionately.

Why are there racist people?

I'm glad that student asked me this question. It is a question we should all ask. Racism is wrong. It is important to condemn it, but it is also important to think critically and ask where racism comes from. If we do that, we may find that someone who is being racist has more in common with us than with the charlatans who have led that person to act that way.

When I share the book *Separate Is Never Equal* with students, a transformation sometimes happens. Kids who thought of each other as different or strange start seeing each other as allies. Sometimes young Latinxs believe that racism and civil rights only involve African Americans. Sometimes African Americans think the current political obsession with a border wall does not affect them. But by learning about each other's struggles—whether through books or by talking and spending time together—we can start to see that we are more alike than different. Recognizing our similarities is a powerful way to combat prejudice.

# NEVER BE AFRAID TO SOAR

by Valerie Wilson Wesley

illustrated by Don Tate

## For My Grandson

You are my one and only. My *grand* boy. I marvel at your strength and skills. I'm proud of how you look out for little kids and how they look up to you. I love to watch you curl up with a book, score the winning point in a game, come up with corny jokes that make everybody laugh. You have a kind, generous heart and a mind that's big enough to swallow the whole world. I know you will do this.

I also know the dangers of growing up in a country that is fearful of the power of black men, that doesn't appreciate their beauty or value their lives. Sometimes I'm afraid that the older you get, the more vulnerable you'll become. I worry that you'll be limited by those who can't see your potential, and you'll be kept from climbing as high as you can go. Whenever that happens, I want you to remember the legacy that your great-grandfather—my father, Bertram W. Wilson, who soared very high—left you.

He was a Tuskegee Airman, and such a great pilot that he won the Distinguished Flying Cross, the highest honor a pilot can receive. When he was your age, he

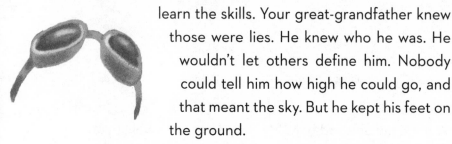

dreamed of flying, but everyone told him it was impossible. Black people weren't allowed to fly planes. Some said we weren't smart enough and couldn't learn the skills. Your great-grandfather knew those were lies. He knew who he was. He wouldn't let others define him. Nobody could tell him how high he could go, and that meant the sky. But he kept his feet on the ground.

Once, when I was a girl and we were driving home, a state trooper pulled us over. He was mean and disrespectful. Your great-grandfather had beautiful, graceful hands that could play the piano, cook gourmet meals, and fly airplanes. The trooper, who probably hated music and *certainly* couldn't fly a plane, didn't see your great-grandfather's many talents. All the officer saw was a black man driving a nice car he didn't think he should own. My father hadn't done anything wrong, yet the trooper had the law on his side and could hurt us both if he wanted to. But your great-grandfather was a war hero and understood what a real battle was. He wasn't about to be goaded into a fight he knew he couldn't win.

I was scared. Your great-grandfather was not. He was angry. I could tell because his jaw was clenched. But your great-grandfather stayed calm and strong. Just like he'd been when he shot down all those Nazi planes to help our country win the war. Just like he'd been when they pinned the medals on his chest. He let the man read his license and write him a ticket. After the trooper had gone, he shook his head, as if dismissing him, and gave me a sad, tired smile. We didn't talk much on the way home, but I knew how brave my father was and that the trooper wasn't worthy of any respect.

That was over sixty years ago, and not much has changed. Black men still get stopped by the police and pulled over for no reason. Sometimes they are killed. We have endured—and will endure—many injustices, but we can't let those stop us from being the best we can be.

We made this country into what it is. Its wealth and power were built on the labor, anguish, and tears of our ancestors, those who were enslaved and those who weren't. Each gift our country has given the world—music, art, food, style—has been graced and made more beautiful by us.

So remember your great-grandfather's lessons and those of other strong black men: Choose your battles wisely. Don't let anyone tell you who you are. Never be goaded into doing foolish things. Remember what has come before and what you must pass on. And *never* be afraid to soar.

# MY OLMEC

by Selina Alko

In the beginning, you slept.
I held you, baby boy, in all of your quiet,
The silence of sleep and peace resting on
    your Olmec face,
A round mask, like the stone heads from
    Central America,
Ancient artisans from long ago,
Holding wisdom and forgotten stories from
    the past,
Outsized hopes and overcast dreams from
    beneath the curtain of your closed eyes,
Your father's complicated African
    American history, mostly unknown.
And from my Canadian side, your Jewish
    lineage—Polish and Latvian with
    tumultuous Turkish roots.

In my arms, you bore your multicultural
    ancestry out loud.
Proud.

Gradually your Olmec face—graceful and
    majestic—began to fill out.

As you grew, carrying quiet confidence and
     keen observation,
     you demonstrated a gift—
The ability to form in your head pictures so
     true to life—
And then you transferred those visions to
     paper.

I watched you navigate the world of two
     cultures,
Translating the music you love into portraits,
Rendering rap and hip-hop artists in
     graphite.
Connecting you to your pops.
Helping you understand a part of yourself.

I wonder if, son,
As a light-skinned brown boy living in
     bougie Brooklyn, you drew to
     self-soothe?
To reflect a growing awareness,
The uneasy truth about growing up mixed-
     race in a racist land.

I, myself, came late to understanding
     racism.
When I married your father, I was largely
     naive.

Coming from Canada, I didn't know much
    about slavery.
Or the Great Migration.
Or Jim Crow.
Or Civil Rights.

Then I learned about Mildred and
    Richard Loving—
An interracial couple living in Virginia in the
    1950s.
They were arrested for their illegal marriage.
Nine years later, they won the right to their
    love.
Only after writing a book about the
    Lovings, I finally understand America's
    sordid past.
How even after slavery ended, laws kept
    Blacks and whites separate.
I saw our family's story in the Lovings'
    story.
And I finally understood.
Only fifty years ago, you, my son, would
    have been born a crime.

Your father says that his whole life was
    "The Talk."
That his single mother overprotected him by
    keeping him indoors.

Sheltering you is not an option for me, your
    white, Jewish mother.
I do not want to raise you to be afraid.
But I do want you to be aware.
I want to help you grow.
I want to help you move through the world
    outside.
Out loud.

Proud.

Now, son.
You are fourteen. A quiet storm.
Are you aware that you may be
    perceived as a threat?
You slam doors and shut me out,
    sleeping half the day away.
When you draw, you astound.
You are winning awards for your art.
I know you are good.
You know you are good.
But does the world see you as good?
You are a teenager.
A wild child, ripe with rebellion.
Olmec eyes of coal.
Wide-set.
All-seeing.
Five feet five inches of brown-boy tall.

So, son.
Do not give them an excuse.
Do not wear a hoodie.
Do not keep your hands inside your pockets.
And, please know.
Please take to heart this truth, my son.
You cannot hide from prejudiced eyes.
But you can move through the world
    outside.
Out loud.

Proud.

# F.R.I.E.N.D.S.
## LOOKING BACK,
## LOOKING FORWARD

by **Torrey Maldonado**

illustrated by **Natacha Bustos**

Dear Ava,

As my daughter, you further our family's journey. Our past will help you rise because it helped me.

We're "Brooklyn"—born and raised—like Miles Morales in *Into the Spider-Verse*. He mirrors the segregated projects and home where I'm from, African American and Puerto Rican.

Nas and Lin-Manuel Miranda echo my rough rise in "I Wrote My Way Out." Nas raps, "Flickerin' lights inside my project hall," and that's Red Hook. Smoky, crumbling, littered stairwells. Uninviting faces and crews. Constant violence and bullying. Shootings shattering lives and futures. *Life* magazine called Red Hook "the crack capital of America."

I was jumped by kids and once by family. Why? The nail that sticks out gets hammered. There, "difference" gets attacked, hammered into conforming.

Daily oppressions made Blacks and Latinos in our projects equals—sharing equal pains and dreams. Brief escapes existed. But it was my mom who offered lasting rescues.

Sometimes I joke, "I had a summertime dad. He was around summa the time." He'd fade in and out of our lives. My mom? She's "no joke." I give her Father's *and* Mother's Day cards; she stood strong as both parents. Hard as a rock, as soft-spoken as Star Wars's Yoda, she told me, "Education and literacy are weapons." She thought they'd help me live the American Dream.

A roadblock? My elementary school failed so many kids, it got shut down. Not before it damaged me, convincing me I was worthless and should wear a dunce cap. Educators mirrored outside bullies, hammering anyone different into one mold. Instead of helping me rise, they made me repeat the third grade. After my holdover year, they tried holding me back again.

School helped to oppress us. Literacy there erased or reduced us. I quit seeing my mom's vision, wondering, *How's the future good when life's always scary?*

My chances to rise were being shattered. But my mom picked up the pieces, personifying that Destiny's Child lyric: "I'm a survivor. I'm not gon' give up." She got my sisters and community to be friends of her dream. With smiling eyes, she'd read to me, teaching me what school didn't. One favorite was *The Snowy Day* by Ezra Jack Keats. Only Tupac's "Keep Ya Head Up" explains the impact of her read-alouds: "Suddenly the ghetto didn't seem so tough. And though we had it rough, we always had enough." She chose books that showed that our block held magic, with messages that could help me rise.

Ma fought to switch my schools. Educators tried killing the transfer, undermining her confidence: "Who do you think you are?" She replied, "His mother!" She taught my older sisters to fight for me. "Who you?" bullies asked, undermining their right to step in. "We're his sisters!"

They stood up for me in ways I couldn't, until I could. They encouraged me to do hard things. My mom: "You *will* sit and read for twenty minutes, then write me a summary!" My sisters made me face bullies: "You fightin' or I'm embarrassin' you." They built resilience that helped me rise.

As kids, one sister and I sang this old-school Whodini rap-verse: "Friends. How many of us have them?" When I got older, an internet acronym of F.R.I.E.N.D.S. made me realize my mom and sisters were my *best* friends.

**F**ight for you

**R**espect you

**I**nclude you

**E**ncourage you

**N**eed you

**D**eserve you

**S**tand by you

In all stages of life, friends, groups, and institutions may be as oppressive as bullies. Sometimes today feels like a global ghetto. Red Hook injustices happen everywhere. The media reveals a rise in uninviting faces, violence, bullying, shootings, unfair incarcerations, failing schools, uncertainties, fears, and more.

How can you help yourself and others rise? Remember our family's rise in the projects: you can rise *anywhere*. Remember my mom personifying "I'm a survivor. I'm not gon' give up."

Also, find sisters like mine. Since you don't have blood siblings, here's how you do it. Keep close family

and friends who do that F.R.I.E.N.D.S. acronym for you. Those are sisters and brothers. Some call them allies or accomplices.

Now I'm an adult. I've used my classroom for twenty years to be the type of educator I needed as a kid. I also write books that the young me needed. I share my mom's vision: education and literacy are weapons that help us rise and resist.

My hope is that you further our family's journey and use our past to rise, too.

I love you,
Daddy

# TEN

by Tracey Baptiste

illustrated by April Harrison

"**B**ecause the lights are flashing behind us, I need to tell you some things. . . .

The first has to do with your face. Keep it neutral."

"What does that mean?" you ask.

"Smile," I say. "Not too much. Try to relax."

We move over to the side, and I stop the car.

"Why did they pull us over?" you want to know.

"We'll find out when they come to us."

"It's taking a while. Maybe we should go find out what they want."

"No. Never. Do not leave the car. Wait. That's the second thing."

The police car door opens. Someone is coming now.

"Okay, third. Hands on the wheel, in your lap, or on the dash where they can see them. Open and flat. Yes. Just like that."

"Ma'am?" the officer asks.

"Sir? What did I do?"

You notice that my tone is even. Questioning, but calm.

That's the fourth thing.

"You were driving a little erratically there. I just wanted to make sure that you're not drinking."

73

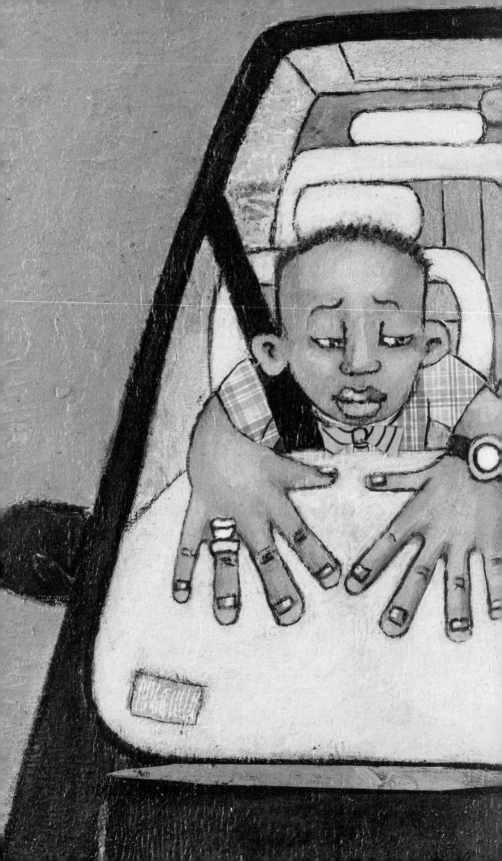

The officer shines a light into the car. He sees you.

"Only juice boxes," I joke.

I laugh. You laugh. He laughs.

That's the fifth thing. To be pleasant.

"License and registration," he says.

I reach into the glove box for the registration. You helpfully open my purse and rifle through for my wallet.

"Thank you, baby," I say.

"I can't find it, Ma."

"Take your time. There's no rush."

You nod. You understand this is number six.

The officer shifts his weight to the other leg. One hand is at his hip. The hilt of his gun is black and shiny.

"Got it!" you shout. You brandish the wallet, grinning.

And then you see my face. You remember to slow down.

I take the wallet slowly, get out the license, and hand it over.

The officer takes both and walks to the squad car.

"What now, Ma?"

"We wait." That's the seventh thing.

"It's taking too long."

"It takes as long as it's going to take."

"I'm hungry."

"We'll be done soon."

"He's coming back," you say. You have twisted your whole body to look at him through the window.

"Sit straight, baby. That's eight."

The officer hands me the license and registration, and you help to put them away.

He looks into the car again. "Careful with those juice boxes," he says with a laugh. "And watch the road. You were swerving a bit there."

The officer returns to his car.

"We can go now, Ma," you say. "Why aren't you driving?"

"That's nine. We don't pull off too fast, okay?"

"Okay."

After a few seconds, we pull away slowly and move down the road.

"What's ten?" you ask. "There are always ten things on a list."

"Ten? Remember who you have at home. Remember that what's important is doing all of the things you need to so you can get back to them. That's ten."

You nod and repeat it. "Ten."

You put your hand in mine. We are nearly home.

# I'M A DANCER

by **Sharon Dennis Wyeth**

illustrated by **Raul Colón**

'm in first grade at a new school, in a new neighborhood, in Washington, D.C., and my class is having a circus. It's near the end of the year, but I'm a newcomer. That day, all the kids are in costume and some of the parents are there, mainly mothers. My mother took time off from work so that she could be with me, too. I also have a costume, a frilly green dress with a short skirt and shiny sequins. It's my wood nymph costume from the kindergarten play at my old school.

"Today my class is having a circus," I reminded my mother when I was getting dressed at home. "This costume is for a wood nymph."

"It doesn't have to be for a wood nymph," Mama assured me. "It can be a dancer's costume."

"Are there dancers in the circus?" I asked, standing taller on my toes.

Mama nodded.

"I like to dance!" I said, practicing my twirl.

Mama smiled. "In your sparkly green costume, you'll fit right in."

When I walk into school with my mother that day, I feel happy and very excited. Everyone is laughing and talking, and the other children's costumes are fun to look at—one boy is dressed up like a tiger! He even has a tail. When he runs around the room showing off his tail and growling, it makes me laugh. And there are refreshments—punch and cookies!

My mother pours me some punch, and I stand next to her and drink it. Some other kids are at the table, too, eating cookies and standing next to their mothers. My new teacher is also there. I notice how tall she is. I think being tall is nice, and I like the way she parts her hair to the side, just like I do.

But today my teacher looks worried. My mother has a worried look, too, and I wonder why. Today is a happy day. We're having a circus! I turn to one of the other mothers.

"I'm a dancer," I say, pointing to my costume. I look up at her eyes and smile.

But the other mother doesn't smile back. Instead, she takes her child's hand and walks away. Then, one by one, all the other mothers walk away, too, with their children. I'm confused. I begin to twirl around and around.

"I'm a dancer!" I cry, hoping they'll hear me. "I'm a dancer!"

But by now, everyone except my own mother, my new teacher, and me are on the other side of the room.

My mother takes my hand and smiles sadly. My new teacher looks sad, too.

Then the new teacher says in a voice I can barely hear: "Very nice . . ."

And then she, too, walks across the room.

My mother and I are left standing alone while the other mothers talk among themselves and my new classmates drink punch and laugh and run around, having fun in their costumes. I settle down on the floor next to my mother's feet, munching a cookie, and no one comes near us. It's as if my mother and I are in a special circle where we've become invisible. . . .

The year is 1955. Last year, before integration, I wouldn't have been allowed to attend my new school, because only White children were allowed to go there. But in first grade, I know nothing about all that. What I do know is that when I smile at home, the people in my family smile back. When I speak, they listen. But that day, the parents of my new classmates ignore my mother and me. They pretend we aren't even there. And I feel it. At the classroom circus at my new school, I feel cut off and set apart.

My mother takes me out of school early. I'm still wearing my costume, and instead of feeling pretty, now it feels sticky.

"You're very quiet," my mother says, squeezing my hand. "Are you okay?"

"I have a tummy ache," I tell her.

"I'm sorry," she says softly. "I guess that circus wasn't much fun."

We walk the rest of the way in silence. . . .

My mother didn't try to explain what happened in the classroom. Maybe she thought I was too young to understand. Or maybe she didn't want to hurt me. How do you break the news to your precious child that some people might not want her around because she and her family are Negro? When I got older and knew what racism was, the two of us had long talks. But that day in first grade, it was more about what my mother did when we got home than what she said.

When we got back to the apartment, she put on a classical record, *Sleeping Beauty* by Tchaikovsky.

"Would you like to dance?" she asked.

I shook my head. "My tummy still aches a little."

"I'll dance with you," she offered. She gently pulled me onto the living room floor, and the two of us began to dance. Mama lifted her arms, and I lifted mine. We started to skip and glide.

Happiness filled my heart, and I forgot all about my tummy.

Mama stood back for a minute as I twirled.

"That's more like it!" she called over the sound of the music. "Don't ever let anyone take away your joy!"

In my life, there would be times when I encountered racism that was more obvious. When I was in a Shakespeare play in my integrated high school, a boy's mother pulled him out because she didn't want her son to act onstage with me. I was supposed to play Juliet, and my White classmate was supposed to play Romeo. I was shocked when I got the news that my White classmate's mother was upset. Her son had seemed happy to get the part. But his mother told the teachers in charge that as long as a Negro girl was Juliet, her son could not be Romeo. When I went home and told my mother, she asked me how I felt.

"It hurts my feelings," I confessed. "But I feel sorry for my classmate. His mother told him he couldn't be Romeo, all because of prejudice. But nobody's going to stop me from playing Juliet!"

"Good girl," said my mother.

I hadn't forgotten her wise words on that day when I went to my new first-grade class, wearing my sparkly costume. I'd wanted to join in the fun, but my mother and I were excluded. I'd wanted to dance for my classmates and their mothers, but I was ignored.

"Don't ever let anyone take away your joy!" my mother told me.

I still dance today. No one can stop me.

# HABLAR

by Meg Medina

illustrated by Rudy Gutierrez

I was thinking about when you were really little. Do you remember? You sat squirming in my lap as we read books about animals, which were your favorite because we copied their sounds and giggled until it was time to sleep. In no time, you knew that a rooster can say *qui quiri qui* or *cock-a-doodle doo*. It's still the same bird. A puppy can say *ruff ruff* or *jau jau jau*. Either way, its fur is warm to cuddle close.

It's the same for people like us, too, mi amor. Your mouth is filled with words you learned from us, in English and en español, words flowing from one river to the next, getting wider and deeper, gathering speed as they joined inside you. We gave you those palabras so that you'd know the sound of your abuelas and their mothers before that, the ones who dared to dream and came searching for a new place to call home. We gave you those words so that you wouldn't forget where you began.

Mira, mi amor, the talk I'm giving you now is about how others hear those words. I want you to be ready because sometimes our words will give you trouble.

Here is a fact, corazón. You will hear other words— palabras feas—that might sound like this:

English only! This is America! Speak our language!

You'll hear them when you least expect it, and sometimes you may wonder if you really heard them at all. They'll float out from the TV news as you're doing your homework. Or they'll fall from the mouth of an adult you thought you could trust at school. You might hear them from a lady who's shopping near us, even if it is only with her suspicious eyes as we chat. You will meet people who will tell you that your words are something you should do in private, like an ugly secret. They will not want to translate for someone who doesn't understand. They will treat your sounds as something foreign that offends and separates. They will say it does not belong here if you want to succeed.

Mi amor, I know that those words will make your mouth turn into a sinking stone and pull your eyes to your shoes. You may decide that it's easier to let español be dragged from you so that you do not invite something worse. It will be tempting to answer me in English and act as American as apple pie. You may even wonder if maybe they're right.

Pero mira, mi vida, at those times I want you to think of me and all those days we read. Español was given to you in your American cradle for a reason. It is what binds you to all that has come before and to all the hard journeys that were made to get us here. It is the language

90

of our roots, strength, and survival. It is our history, and no matter what others may tell you, it is this country's history, too.

Mi corazón, sometimes you'll have to be brave to show everyone who you are. Don't be ashamed. Our words *are* beautiful. Our words belong here. They give you more ways to understand people around you. We blessed you with them so that you could give and receive more love from this big and colorful world.

Remember that no language is better than another. No tongue makes one person more real or more important than someone else. And no great country ever tried to silence its people or make them all the same.

# OUR INHERITANCE

by Adam Gidwitz

illustrated by Peter H. Reynolds

My daughter and I are sitting on the roof of our home in Brooklyn Heights. It's a fine summer day. We're looking out over the water, at the glass buildings of Manhattan, reflecting the sun. The glass of the buildings and the water of the harbor are a million different shades of blue.

My daughter is in fourth grade. It is six years in the future.

She says, "Do you think there are still racists, Daddy?"

I have to admit, I'm surprised by the question. I say, "Why do you ask?"

"Because being racist is stupid. The color of your skin has nothing to do with how smart you are or how good you are."

"Preach, girl."

"So . . . *is* there still racism?"

"Oh, yes. All over the place."

"What? But we don't *know* any racists, right? We're not *friends* with any, are we?" And then she decides, "We wouldn't be."

I look at my beautiful daughter. I say, "I think the word 'racism' means a lot more than just 'thinking someone is worse because of their skin color.' That's one kind of racism. But it isn't the only kind. It isn't the most common kind, either."

"What other kinds are there?"

"You know the story of Papa Jake? Your great-great-grandfather?"

"Yes. I like that story."

So I tell it:

Papa Jake was the first of our family in this country. He came over as a teenager in about 1880, all by himself—a Jewish immigrant boy who barely spoke English. He traveled to Mississippi, where he sold pots and pans by hauling a cart under the hot sun. Eventually, he opened a hardware store. The store was very successful.

Now, not everyone down in Mississippi liked him. He was a little Jewish man with a heavy accent. There was one guy, who owned another hardware store in the same town, who *hated* Papa Jake. He was always ragging on him for being Jewish, teasing him, calling him ugly names.

My daughter interrupts the story. "*That* guy was a racist."

"Yes, he was."

One day, this racist was saying such awful things to Papa Jake that your great-great-grandfather walked straight up to the racist and punched him once, right on the chin. Knocked him out cold. One punch.

My daughter grins. I can see her little hands are fists. "Papa Jake was cool."

"He was certainly a tough little guy. But have you ever thought about what would have happened if Papa Jake had been a black man? And punched out that white racist shop owner?"

She shrugs and shakes her head.

"He could have been lynched—hanged, without a trial, from a tree. Or beaten. Or shot. What *did* happen to Papa Jake?"

"Not that."

"No. Nothing."

I go on: "Eventually, Papa Jake had three sons. He gave them each some money, and they started a little shampoo company. That shampoo company grew and grew into one of the biggest shampoo companies in the whole country.

"We still have the money from that shampoo company. That money is what let us buy this nice house; that money is what lets us live in this neighborhood; that money is what let me quit my job as a teacher and take a risk on becoming a writer."

"Okay," says my daughter. "So that shop owner was racist. And Papa Jake didn't get lynched. He was lucky, I guess. So . . . who are our racist friends? That's what you were supposed to be telling me."

"Yeah, I *know*," I say, rolling my eyes. "Everything I just told you about Papa Jake is true. You've heard that story before. But it's not the *whole* story."

A nervous silence falls over my daughter. The pinks have turned to grays, the oranges to blues.

"When Papa Jake opened that store in Mississippi, it was about twenty-five years after the enslaved people had been freed. But most weren't *really* free. They lived in the same slave houses, worked the same land, often for the same slave owners. The only difference was that they were called sharecroppers, and they were kept on the land not by law, but by *debt*. So slavery, really, continued for many more decades. It just had a different name. Sharecropping.

"Well, most of Papa Jake's customers were sharecroppers. Since they were kept poor by debt, they always paid Papa Jake with credit. So they were in debt to him, too.

"Eventually, Papa Jake was owed so much money by his sharecropper customers that he got to take possession of the land that a group of them lived on. He evicted a bunch of those families—kicked them out of their homes."

My daughter's eyes go wide at that.

"Other families he let stay. Papa Jake made so much money from that land that he bought some more. Pretty soon, he owned most of the land in that county. Which means there must have been hundreds of share-croppers working his land, stuck there like slaves, trapped by debt . . . to him.

"And *that's* how Papa Jake made the money that he gave his sons to start that shampoo company. Not from a little hardware store. Little hardware stores don't make that kind of money. It was from the labor of those proud black women, men, and children who, decades after slavery, were still enslaved . . . by our Papa Jake."

The harbor is dark now. My daughter moves away from me. To the edge of our building. Ferries, lit by strings of lights, stream across the evening. "But," she says, "but . . ."

"But that's not *us*," I say. "*We* didn't do that."

"Right!" she says, relieved.

"That is true, sweetie. We did not. We would not. But it's easy to say that. Now that we have this beautiful home that sharecropping money helped pay for. Now that I can be a successful writer—because I had Papa Jake's money to help me get started."

I scooch myself forward to sit beside her. "Look at this gorgeous harbor. The most perfect natural harbor in

North America. Look at those towering buildings across the water. Look at our beautiful neighborhood."

She looks. The streets around us are lined with stately brick homes, all shadow and gaslight. I say:

"We live on land that belonged to Lenape Indians, land that was taken from them. Land that was worked by indentured servants and slaves. In a nation that wrote slavery of Africans into its Constitution and the genocide of Native Americans into its Declaration of Independence. In a city that grew rich from importing Southern cotton, grown by the enslaved. In a neighborhood built by bankers and shippers and speculators whose best investments were slaves and the produce of slave labor, as well as the stealing and exploitation of Native land. Wall Street, right across the water there, is the site of the New York City slave auction. That's no coincidence." I put a fist on my daughter's knee. She looks at it. I say, "Racism is not just hatred. Racism is a system. A system that dehumanizes humans in order to keep them down and, most often, to make money off of them."

My daughter exhales. I wonder if she regrets starting this whole conversation. But she hasn't left yet. Hasn't gone downstairs to hide from her discomfort in the soft light of small screens. For that, I'm proud of her.

I ask, "Are we polluters?"

She's very eco-conscious, so I know what she's going to say. She crinkles her chin. "Yeah. We recycle, and we reuse. We're not a big coal plant, pumping poison into the sky. But we use plastic, we use cars, we fly when we go on vacation. We're polluters. I wish we weren't."

I smile at her sadly. "You're so smart."

My daughter turns and faces me.

I say: "Being a polluter is a lot like being a racist. I hate pollution. And I hate racism. But I sit here and I benefit from them both."

She squints. I tell her, "My country was built on racism. My *life* was built on it. You asked me, 'Who are the racists that we know?' I am sorry to tell you: You're looking at one right now."

There is silence. Around us, the sky is black. The moon shines down brightly, amid a near-starless sky.

"I try to fight racism every day, sweetheart. I try to understand a system that *still* treats people unfairly—that segregates our neighborhoods, that keeps resources in white hands. And I try to change that system, to make it more fair to everyone. But being racist isn't *some other people's* problem. It's *mine*. And, though I've tried so hard to raise you right, it's yours, too."

My daughter asks, "What are you saying?"

"Only this: I want you to be honest with yourself about our inheritance—our inheritance of racism. Learn about it. Think about it. Maybe one day you'll want to join the people who are working to fight racism in our society. I hope you do. But the first step, the most important step, is being honest. Learning, and being uncomfortable with what you learn, and most of all, being honest. And then, when *you* have a child, and you have this talk with *them,* maybe we'll be living in a more fair and just world. And maybe, just maybe, you'll be able to say that you helped make it that way."

# TOUGH TUESDAY

by Nikki Grimes

illustrated by Erin K. Robinson

The morning seemed serene,
sun scattering its rays,
sky blue enough to swim in,
just like the day before.
I rang my friend's doorbell,
waited for the wordless hello
of her smile.
The door swung wide
and on the other side
stood her rarely-at-home daddy,
snarling down at me,
his neck and eyes
a screaming red.
"Nigger, get off my porch!" he said.
"And don't come 'round again!"

Too stunned to cry,
I turned away,
but not before I
spied my friend
through the screen door,
hunched in the hall,
draped in silence.

Sorrow blinding me,
I stumbled home,
straight into the blanket
of my mother's arms.
"Some folk will always
call you outside your name,"
she explained.
"Honey,
you can't stop hateful people
slinging hurtful words
like stones.
But who says
you have to pick them up
and put them in your pocket?"
In my heart,
the answer slowly sprouted:
    *Not me.*
       *Not Me.*
          *NOT ME!*

# THE ROAD AHEAD

by Minh Lê

illustrated by Cozbi A. Cabrera

**THIS IS ABOUT MORE THAN JUST TAKING CARE OF YOURSELF—IT'S ABOUT STAYING ALERT TO EVERY-THING AROUND YOU AND BEING RESPONSIBLE FOR THE WELL-BEING OF OTHERS.**

My mom and dad (your grandparents) did most of their parenting by example, so while they gently guided me and my sisters through the twists and turns of childhood, I actually don't remember having "the talk."

But there is a talk that I've found useful for making sense of the world . . . from when your grandfather taught me how to drive.

When I was your age, I couldn't wait to get on the road. In fact, my sisters and I used to sneak into the garage, climb into the oversized driver's seats, and make vrooming sounds as we pretended to race. But when the time came to actually drive, before letting me get behind the wheel, my dad stressed that being truly responsible meant thinking about more than just yourself. You have to always be alert to potential threats: that car drifting between lanes, the patch of black ice, your own blind spots.

In short: a good driver is a mindful driver.

That lesson has somehow stuck with me. Not only because mindfulness is something that both of your grandparents emphasized but also because now, as a writer, I am hopelessly drawn to metaphor. So I lean on this talk as a kind of guide for navigating the world—even when I'm not in a car.

Moving through life as a responsible member of society requires an intense alertness. Threats, visible and invisible, could be lurking around any corner. As a kid, I took that to heart, but now, as a parent, the stakes have changed. When I look in the rearview mirror and see your peaceful faces asleep in the backseat, I find myself asking:

*How do I protect your innocence while also preparing you for life's harsh realities?*

As I write this, you are seven and four years old, and are two totally magical little souls. Which is why I'm shaken knowing that there are people who may wish you harm simply because of your heritage and who you are. While society has made important progress in many areas, it sadly feels like we are currently trending in the wrong direction.

I am Vietnamese American, and your mom is white. While things could be worse (it wasn't all that long ago that our relationship would have been illegal), there are still places where our beautiful mixed-race family draws threatening looks.

I am Buddhist, and your mom is Jewish. While we will always rejoice in this blending of faiths, spirituality can feel tenuous when the headlines are riddled with attacks on places of worship.

We also come from a family of immigrants and refugees. I am very proud of this history, but we live in a time when racist vitriol is trumpeted from the highest offices, emboldening a dark nationalistic rage that had been festering in the shadows.

So now at bedtime, when you ask "Are bad guys real?" I think: *Do I tell you the truth? That the world is full of wonders but is also home to darkness?*

Your innocence feels so precious, and I want to preserve that for as long as possible. But you can see the world outside your windows.

Recently, after yet another synagogue shooting, your mom and I avoided the news to shield you both from the tragic details. But when we pulled up to our own synagogue, we felt our hearts break as one of you asked from the backseat, "Why do we need police at temple?"

And while I want you to be aware of potential danger, you have also been born with tremendous privileges, things that could make you unaware of other people's struggles. We all have important issues that we are initially unaware of, but it is our responsibility to learn. Obliviousness is not an excuse.

When you do take driving lessons, they won't tell you that checking your blind spots is optional. No, it is your responsibility. The same goes for the world at large: It is our responsibility to stay awake and aware, to do our best to see and understand what is not in our immediate line of sight and to grasp those things that are not immediately apparant to us. Failing to fully check yourself and your surroundings makes *you* the danger on and off the road.

III

It's hard to believe, but soon enough it will be your turn to get behind the wheel. And while I want to prepare you to be alert, conscientious, and engaged, I also desperately want you, and all children, to have the freedom to just *be*. I used to think that was a contradiction, that it wasn't possible to be both cautious and joyous. But now I realize that being alert to the world's darkness also means that your eyes are more open to its dazzling beauty.

I love you both so much, and as you continue on your journey, I hope you will take it all in—the darkness and the light. And my wish for you is that by being mindful, you will be able to look out upon the horizon with clarity and hope, roll down the windows, turn up the music, and feel the wind in your hair as you hurtle forward into the future.

# MAZES

by Christopher Myers

There is a story. It is one of the oldest stories.

First there are monsters.
Then heroes come along. They smile.
They speak and try hard.
And they slay the monsters.

Repeat as necessary.

These are the rules.

The newspapers show blurry photos of us. The headlines say words like "Outrage!" or "Attack!"

Reporters do interviews, and people say, "I don't really know what happened . . . ," before they tell whatever story they have been told to say. "We were just sitting there minding our business and . . ."

This story has been told before, since before before. Always the same.

Politicians promise to look into ways of slaying the monsters. They make committees, they appropriate funds. They give speeches, they formulate plans. They call on the heroes, as if they had heroes waiting in their back pockets. Or worse, when they think that they are the heroes: "I will fix these monsters!"

Because they know how the story goes.

Monsters come first, of course. Because the only way to be a hero is to slay one of us.

"So what makes a monster?" you might ask. People who have not given this a lot of thought will say almost anything.

Medusa had snakes for hair. If you are very big, like Godzilla or King Kong. Or very small, like those dolls that come to life in scary movies. If you have skin made of scales, or fur, or some special color. If you have a power, like you are fast, or smart, or can see very well. Laser eyes, for sure. A beard, if it's really bushy, used to be a monster thing. Sometimes monsters can look like regular people—maybe most of the time nowadays.

What really makes a monster, before all of the outside things, is the story.

So, before the hero, there is the monster, and before the monster, there is the story.

⌣

We were monsters before, when they were writing the stories. There was one of us, they called him the Minotaur, though his name was Asterion. And each year the people—who called themselves the people because they imagined themselves to be simple and easy to define like that—they would sacrifice fourteen children to this Minotaur. They killed the children and laid their bodies at the doorway to the vast maze that was the Minotaur's home.

I know you are thinking this is a horrific thing to do, to hurt children. You are right. But these people were so eager to have a monster that they even provided the horrific acts to put in the monster's name. You will find this over and over again, when people do bad things and accuse the monster of doing these things.

Some of the things you will hear about the Minotaur are true. Things will feel familiar, because he was one of us. He had horns, great wide horns that looked as if a sliver of the moon had landed on his head, like yours or mine. He lived in a maze because, like all of us, he had an amazing sense of direction and a love for discovery, for everyday journeys, and for tight spaces that open up into great rooms.

Most of the things you will hear about the Minotaur are lies. The people say he was bloodthirsty. This makes very little sense, as we are all vegetarians like our bovine cousins. (Who has ever heard of a bloodthirsty cow?) The people say he demanded a sacrifice. That he lived in the maze to trap unsuspecting travelers.
So many lies, just to make a better monster of him.

I suspect they told these stories, to make themselves heroes. And I wish they could have made themselves heroes some better way. If they could choose their monsters without involving us.

But they always do. Minotaurs or Hydra, foreign hordes, creeping perils, hidden dangers, all of them, all of us, some sort of monster in their hero factory.

Asterion cried and cried as he picked up the children's bodies, as he cleaned off their faces, and tried his best to tell the little memory of each child that someone had once loved it, though he could not speak the people's language, and they were children of the people.

The people wrote newspaper articles and held rallies. They made horrific drawings of Asterion carrying the

bodies. Until one of them, one of the people, thought he would try to kill the monster.

He went into the maze. He left a trail for himself with a spool of golden thread. He entered the labyrinth, which was Asterion's home, with sharp weapons, a short tongue, and steel in his eye. He chased Asterion down, and killed him.

The people cheered. They named the killer a king. They paraded Asterion's body around the town.

Even to this day, we still live with the story, you know. Stories have such long ghosts.

A teacher may say something sly, like "I mean, you'd never get lost." Or there would be a joke by a cruel student about sacrifices or parades. One of the people children will put their fingers up by their foreheads and laughingly moo. As if your horns weren't gifts, silver as the moon, handed down from generations. They will try to shame you for your gifts, you know.

And inside you will cry a little. Like Asterion cried. Like all of the monsters before us cried.

And they will try to shame you for your tears, too.

Each shame, every history, all the newspapers and blurry photographs, the headlines and insinuations, the sly comments from well-intentioned teachers, the behind-the-back talking of kids in your school, they all feel like walls to you, borders that crisscross through your heart.

But, if I may remind you—there is some remnant of truth in these stories. All the stories that they try to make into prisons were maybe labyrinths once, like a heritage or a home. Asterion did have fine arcing horns, silver as the moon.

As do you.

Asterion made his home in a maze. There was a comfort with finding his way, a thrill at the daily discovery. That was why he had the architect Daedalus build it that way. Because no maze can lose you, if you know where you belong inside.

And like him, you can find comfort in a maze. Even if they are built of stone walls, or rumors, whispers, blurry photographs, and stories.

In fact, that is what you should know: the stories are mazes. Before there were heroes, or monsters, first

there were stories. And we can write and rewrite these
stories.

We have lived in mazes since before before.
And we will find our ways out of them when they
constrict us.
And we will find our ways into them when we seek their
protection.

Mazes and stories. They are as much a part of you as
those shining silver horns upon your head. And *you* can
be the architect, build and rebuild them.

Shut out the heroes, with their sharp weapons and
steel eyes.
Shut out the villagers and newspapers that forget your
name and call you monster.

You will build a new world for all of us, young one.

⌣

There is a story. It is one of the oldest stories.
It is like a maze, waiting for someone for whom mazes
are home.
For someone to rewrite the borders, the walls, the edges.
To make the story a home for us all.
There is a story.

It is waiting for you.

# SOURCES AND NOTES FROM THE AUTHORS

**Renée Watson**

While there was not room in my story "Remember This" to share the full biographies of the empowering African American women mentioned, additional information about their inspiring works and achievements is included below.

- **Maya Angelou** (1928-2014): poet, singer, activist. At a time when the voices of Black women were often silenced or ignored, Maya wrote poetry that celebrated Black culture and honored the lives of Black women. She spoke six languages and was the second poet in history to recite a poem at a presidential inauguration.
- **Shirley Chisholm** (1924-2005): the first African American woman in Congress and the first woman and African American to seek the nomination for president of the United States. She was an advocate for women and fought for racial and gender equality.
- **Lucille Clifton** (1936-2010): poet who often wrote about body image, womanhood, and family. She published more than sixteen books for children. She believed Black children needed books that reflected their heritage and helped them understand their world.

- **Fannie Lou Hamer** (1917–1977): African American civil rights activist. In 1964, she helped organize Freedom Summer, a movement that brought hundreds of African American and white college students together to help with African American voter registration in the segregated South.

## Derrick Barnes

In "Handle Your Business" I mentioned the four largest African empires (the Egyptian Empire, the Kingdom of Kush, the Mali Empire, and the Songhai Empire). These empires made tremendous contributions to technology and culture that we still benefit from today. Read more about their accomplishments below and online.

**The four largest African empires:**
- Located in North Africa along the lower reaches of the Nile River, the ancient Egyptian Empire (3100 BCE–30 BCE) flourished for several dynasties, ending with their last ruler, Cleopatra VII. Their contributions include developing hieroglyphics as a writing style and the engineering marvel of the pyramids, constructed around 2,500 BCE.
- The Kingdom of Kush (1070 BCE–727 BCE) occupied land in both northeast Africa and to the south of the ancient Egyptians. There is evidence these two civilizations were

in contact with each other starting around c. 3150 BCE. The region was a main source of gold and iron, which provided the kingdom with trading power and metals for weaponry.

- The Mali Empire (800 CE–1550 CE) started in West Africa along the banks of the Niger River before eventually spreading to reach the Atlantic Ocean. The empire's wealth was derived from gold and salt mines. During his 1324 pilgrimage to Mecca, Mali emperor Mansa Mūsā brought as many as sixty thousand soldiers, officials, and attendants with him as well as a hundred camels loaded with gold, which he spent and traded along the route.

- The Songhai Empire (1461 CE–1591 CE) was the largest and the last of the major ancient civilizations and was also concentrated around the Niger River in West Africa. In the capital city of Gao, the Songhai built the Gao mosque and the Tomb of Askia, a monument to their most influential emperor, Askia Mohammad I. The city remains a trading hub to this day.

**Continue discovering more with the following online sources:**

Canós-Donnay, Sirio. "The Empire of Mali." *Oxford Research Encyclopedias*, February 2019. oxfordre.com/ africanhistory/view/10.1093/ acrefore/9780190277734.001.0001/

acrefore-9780190277734-e-266. Accessed
February 1, 2020.

Cartwight, Mark. "Songhai Empire." *Ancient
History Encyclopedia*, March 2019.
www.ancient.eu/Songhai_Empire/.
Accessed January 17, 2020.

Caryl-Sue, National Geographic Society. "The
Kingdoms of Kush." *National Geographic*,
July 2018. www.nationalgeographic.org/
media/kingdoms-kush/. Accessed January
15, 2020.

"The Empire of Mali" (1230–1600). *South African
History Online*, August 2019. www.sahistory
.org.za/article/empire-mali-1230-1600.
Accessed January 15, 2020.

History.com editors. "Ancient Egypt."
History.com, A&E Television Networks,
February 2020. www.history.com/topics/
ancient-history/ancient-egypt. Accessed
January 15, 2020.

Mark, Joshua J. "Egyptian Empire." *Ancient
History Encyclopedia*, September 2017.
www.ancient.eu/Egyptian_Empire/.
Accessed January 17, 2020.

Mark, Joshua J. "The Kingdom of Kush." *Ancient
History Encyclopedia*, February 2018.
www.ancient.eu/Kush/. Accessed January
17, 2020.

Tesfu, Julianna. "Songhai Empire (Ca. 1375–1591)."
     BlackPast, June 2008. www.blackpast
     .org/global-african-history/songhai
     -empire-ca-1375-1591/. Accessed February 1,
     2020.
UShistory.org. "Ancient Egypt." *Ancient
     Civilizations Online Textbook,* 2020.
     www.ushistory.org/civ/3.asp. Accessed
     January 15, 2020.
UShistory.org. "Mali: A Cultural Center." *Ancient
     Civilizations Online Textbook,* 2020.
     www.ushistory.org/civ/3.asp. Accessed
     January 15, 2020.

## Traci Sorell

"The Way of the Anigiduwagi" only touches on the rich and storied history of the Cherokee people. The homelands of the Cherokee people are found in what is currently the southeastern part of the United States. But the forced removal of most Cherokee in the late 1830s to Indian Territory (what is now northeastern Oklahoma) caused a huge disruption. The teaching of language, traditional culture, and strong family ties through the Cherokee's seven clans suffered when over four thousand citizens died before and during the removal, creating a sizeable orphan population that had never previously existed. Still today, the Cherokee people struggle to counteract the impact of these historic events as they raise the next generation to carry on the traditions, learn the language, and thrive as sovereign Native Nations in the midst of ongoing efforts to assimilate them and undermine their ability to govern.

## Duncan Tonatiuh

When writing "Why Are There Racist People?" the following provided insight and context.

Kornbluth, Jacob, director. *Inequality for All*. Beverly Hills, CA: Anchor Bay Entertainment, 2013.

Kristof, Nicholas. "An Idiot's Guide to Inequality." *The New York Times*, July 23, 2014. www.nytimes.com/2014/07/24/opinion/ nicholas-kristof-idiots-guide-to-inequality -piketty-capital.html

Stiglitz, Joseph E. "Of the 1%, By the 1%, For the 1%." *Vanity Fair*, March 31, 2011. www.vanityfair.com/news/2011/05/ top-one-percent-201105

Zinn, Howard. *A People's History of the United States*. New York: Harper & Row, 1990.

## A Note from Meg Medina About "Hablar"

Although English is the language spoken most widely in the United States, there is no official language in our country. Efforts to designate English as a national language date back to the 1700s, but they have been defeated on the grounds that it would be perilous to the rights of non-English speakers. We are a country of people who have come from all over the world. I encourage readers to embrace this astounding gift. Multilingualism benefits young people in their thinking and reasoning, in reading, and, most importantly, in their ability to empathize. Language is a powerful connector.

# ABOUT THE AUTHORS AND ARTISTS

It is no wonder that award-winning writer-illustrator **Selina Alko** now spends her days melding words and mixed-media art to convey stories of hope and inspiration—as well as an alternative viewpoint. Growing up in Vancouver, British Columbia, with a Turkish father who spoke seven languages and taught painting and a mother who worked in the family's century-old metal recycling business, she was surrounded by the melody of words and stories from different places. Selina's books include *The Case for Loving: The Fight for Interracial Marriage*, *B Is for Brooklyn*, and *Daddy Christmas & Hanukkah Mama*. She lives in Brooklyn, New York, with her multiracial family. **selinaalko.com**

**Tracey Baptiste** is the *New York Times* bestselling author of *Minecraft: The Crash*. She is also the author of the popular Jumbies series, including *The Jumbies*, *Rise of the Jumbies*, and *The Jumbie God's Revenge*. She has written several other fiction and nonfiction books for children. **traceybaptiste.com**

**Derrick Barnes** is from Kansas City, Missouri. He is a graduate of Jackson State University with a BA degree in marketing. His ninth release, *Crown: An Ode to the Fresh Cut*, won two Ezra Jack Keats Awards, two Coretta Scott King Honor Awards, a Newbery Honor, a Caldecott Honor, and the *Kirkus* Prize for Young Readers, making it one of the most decorated picture books in the history of children's literature.

He is also the author of the bestselling chapter book series Ruby and the Booker Boys and the middle-grade classic *We Could Be Brothers*. His tenth release, *The King of Kindergarten*, debuted on the *New York Times* bestseller list.

Prior to becoming a published author, Derrick wrote bestselling copy for various Hallmark Card lines and was the first African American male staff writer for the company. He resides in Charlotte, North Carolina, with his enchanting wife, Dr. Tinka Barnes, and their four sons. **derrickdbarnes.com**

 **Natacha Bustos** is a Spanish comic book artist based in Barcelona who draws for mostly American comics. She drew the story "Going Nowhere" for the third issue of the Vertigo comic *Strange Sports Stories*, written by Brandon Montclare. Bustos made her Marvel debut with *Spider-Woman #10*, and then she became the regular artist for the Moon Girl and Devil Dinosaur series. She is the winner of a Glyph Award for Best Female Character and is known for her cover artwork for BOOM! Studios, including *Lumberjanes/Gotham Academy*, *Saban's Go Go Power Rangers*, *The Thrilling Adventure Hour*, *Jonesy*, and *Slam!* **natachabustos.blogspot.com**

 **Cozbi A. Cabrera** writes and illustrates children's books and designs quilts and clothing. Trained as an art director, this Parsons School of Design grad left her dream job creating music packaging in New York to make handmade collectible cloth dolls (muñecas) in honor of her Honduran heritage. Her creations have been featured on the *Oprah Winfrey Show*, *Martha Stewart Living*, and many U.S. television networks.

Additionally, Cozbi is the writer and illustrator of *My Hair Is a Garden* and the forthcoming *Me & Mama*. Her illustrated titles include *Beauty, Her Basket* by Sandra Belton; *Thanks*

a *Million* by Nikki Grimes; *Stitchin' and Pullin': A Gee's Bend Quilt* by Patricia McKissack; *Most Loved in All the World* by Tonya Cherie Hegamin, which won the Christopher Award; and *Exquisite: The Poetry and Life of Gwendolyn Brooks* by Suzanne Slade. **cozbi.com**

**Raul Colón** was born in New York City and raised in Puerto Rico, where he studied commercial art in high school. While working as an artist for a Fort Lauderdale instructional television center, doing everything from making animated short films to working with puppets, he came to realize that illustration was his true passion. As a freelance illustrator, he has worked for the *New York Times Book Review*, the *New Yorker*, and *New York* magazine. The publishing industry has recognized Raul with a Golden Kite Award, a Pura Belpré Award, and both a gold and silver medal in the Society of Illustrators Original Art show. Raul wrote and illustrated the picture book *Draw!*, which the *New York Times* chose as one of the Ten Best Illustrated Books of the Year. He is also the author-illustrator of the picture book *Imagine!* Raul lives in New York City with his family.

**Adam Gidwitz** is the author of Newbery Honor winner *The Inquisitor's Tale* and the *New York Times* bestseller *A Tale Dark & Grimm* and its companion novels, and he is the coauthor of the bestselling Unicorn Rescue Society series. For each Unicorn Rescue Society novel, Adam teams up with authors like Joseph Bruchac, David Bowles, Emma Otheguy, and Hena Khan to celebrate the world's mythologies and legendary creatures. Adam's contribution to this volume, "Our Inheritance," was inspired in part by a life-changing workshop called "Undoing Racism," offered by the People's

Institute for Survival and Beyond (**pisab.org**). This workshop is offered in cities around the country, and Adam cannot recommend it enough. **adamgidwitz.com**

 *New York Times* bestselling author **Nikki Grimes** is the recipient of the Children's Literature Legacy Award for substantial and lasting contributions to literature for children, the Virginia Hamilton Literary Award, and the NCTE Award for Excellence in Poetry for Children. She is the author of Coretta Scott King Author Award–winner *Bronx Masquerade*, and the Michael L. Printz and Robert F. Sibert Honor book *Ordinary Hazards: A Memoir.* She is the recipient of five Coretta Scott King Author Honors. Her most recent titles include the much-honored *Words with Wings, Garvey's Choice, Between the Lines,* and the *Boston Globe-Horn Book* Honor winner *One Last Word,* which also won a Lee Bennett Hopkins Poetry Award. Nikki lives in Corona, California. **nikkigrimes.com**

 **Rudy Gutierrez** is an American artist/illustrator of Puerto Rican heritage. He is a Pratt Institute graduate, and his art has been published and viewed worldwide. Among his awards are a Caldecott Honor Award, an International Labor Communications Honor, and from the Society of Illustrators, the Dean Cornwell Hall of Fame Award, Distinguished Educator in the Arts Award, and a Gold Medal. His children's book art has garnered him a Pura Belpré Award, an Américas Book Award, an Africana Book Award, a Shining Willow Honor, and a New York Book Award. His paintings have been featured at the Mesa Contemporary Arts Museum in Arizona, at the first anti-apartheid show at the United Nations, and at the World Conference Against Racism in South Africa.

Rudy has lectured at various institutions and teaches at Pratt Institute. **altpick.com/rudygutierrez**

**April Harrison** is a fine artist and an illustrator whose artwork has appeared in galleries in South Carolina, Georgia, Virginia, and New York. She works primarily with acrylics, powders, watercolors, pencil, and collage. April and her art have been featured in print, television, and film, including works by OWN Network. Her work has also appeared in *Essence* magazine, *Upscale* magazine, *Charleston Scene,* and *Greenville Journal.* As an illustrator of children's books, April received the Coretta Scott King–John Steptoe Award for New Talent for her work on the picture book *What Is Given from the Heart* by author Patricia C. McKissack. *Publishers Weekly* gave the title a starred review, calling the artwork "stunning, aesthetically ambitious." She is also the illustrator of *Nana Akua Goes to School* by Tricia Elam Walker. April lives in Greenville, South Carolina. **aprilsonggallery.com**

**Cheryl Willis Hudson** is an author, an editor, and a publisher. She is the cofounder and editorial director of Just Us Books, Inc., an independent company that focuses on Black interest books for young people. Cheryl has written over two dozen books, including *Bright Eyes, Brown Skin* (with Bernette G. Ford), *AFRO-BETS ABC Book, From Where I Stand, Hands Can, Construction Zone, My Friend Maya Loves to Dance,* and *Brave. Black. First.,* published in collaboration with the Smithsonian National Museum of African American History and Culture. Cheryl is also coeditor with her partner, Wade Hudson, of the middle-grade anthology *We Rise, We Resist, We Raise Our Voices,* which was an International Latino Book Award winner and a Jane Addams Peace Association

Honor Book. As a member of the Children's and Young Adult Committee of PEN America, Cheryl serves as diversity consultant to a number of educational publishers. **cherylwillishudson.com**

 **Wade Hudson** is an author, a publisher, and the president and CEO of Just Us Books, Inc., an independent publisher of books for children and young adults. He has published over thirty books, including *We Rise, We Resist, We Raise Our Voices*, an anthology coedited with his wife. In addition, Wade has completed the poetry collection *Journey: Poems* and is currently working on a coming-of-age memoir.

Wade has received a New Jersey Stephen Crane Literary Award, the Ida B. Wells Institutional Leadership Award, and the Madame C. J. Walker Legacy Award and has been inducted into the International Literary Hall of Fame for Writers of African Descent. He also speaks to students and professional groups around the country about his life's journey, writing and publishing, and the importance of diversity and inclusion. Born and raised in Mansfield, Louisiana, Wade lives in East Orange, New Jersey, with his wife, Cheryl. **wadehudson -authorpublisher.com**

 **Gordon C. James** is a Fort Washington, Maryland, native who attended the School of Visual Arts in New York City. As a fine artist, Gordon works to achieve the highest level of beauty. His art has been featured in *International Artist* magazine and is part of the Paul R. Jones Collection. Gordon's illustrations are soulful and technically sound. He is the illustrator of *Crown: An Ode to the Fresh Cut* by Derrick Barnes and *Let 'Er Buck!* by Vaunda Micheaux

Nelson. His work has garnered numerous awards, including a Caldecott Honor, a Coretta Scott King Honor, and a Society of Illustrators Original Art Gold Medal.

Gordon lives in Charlotte, North Carolina, with his wife, Ingrid; their children, Astrid and Gabriel; and their dog, Rascal. **gordoncjames.com**

**Minh Lê** is the award-winning author of *Drawn Together, Let Me Finish!, The Perfect Seat*, and the middle-grade graphic novel *Green Lantern: Legacy*. He has also written about children's literature for NPR, *HuffPost*, and the *New York Times*. An early-childhood policy expert by day, Minh went to Dartmouth College and has a master's in education from Harvard University. When he's not spending time with his wife and kids in their home in San Diego, his favorite place to be is in the middle of a good book. **minhlebooks.com**

**Earl Bradley (E.B.) Lewis** has illustrated over seventy books for children, including *Each Kindness, Talkin' About Bessie*, and *The Other Side*. His illustrations and paintings have been honored with numerous awards, such as the *New York Times* Best Illustrated Book of the Year, *Kirkus Reviews* Best Children's Illustrated Book of the Year, a Golden Kite Honor Award, a Caldecott Honor Award, and five Coretta Scott King Honor Awards.

Inspired by two artist uncles, E.B. displayed artistic promise as early as the third grade. He attended Temple University's Tyler School of Art and discovered that watercolor was his medium of preference. After graduation, he taught art in public schools for twelve years. Presently, E.B. teaches at the

Pennsylvania Academy of the Fine Arts. He is also a member of the Society of Illustrators in New York City and an artist member of Salmagundi Club of New York.

His works are displayed in museums, owned by private collectors, and sold by art galleries throughout the United States and Europe. **eblewis.com**

Before **Grace Lin** was an award-winning and a *New York Times* bestselling author-illustrator of picture books, early readers, and middle-grade novels, she was the only Asian girl (except for her sisters) at her elementary school in upstate New York. That experience, good and bad, has influenced her books—including her Newbery Honor winner, *Where the Mountain Meets the Moon*; her Theodor Seuss Geisel Honor series, Ling & Ting; her National Book Award Finalist, *When the Sea Turned to Silver*; and her Caldecott Honor winner, *A Big Mooncake for Little Star*. It also causes Grace to persevere for diversity as an occasional New England Public Radio commentator, TEDx Talk presenter ("The Windows and Mirrors of Your Child's Bookshelf"), and *PBS NewsHour* video essayist ("What to Do When You Realize Classic Books from Your Childhood Are Racist"). She continues this mission with her two podcasts, *Kids Ask Authors* and *Book Friends Forever*.

In 2016, Grace's art was displayed at the White House, and Grace was recognized by President Obama as a Champion of Change for Asian American and Pacific Islander Art and Storytelling. **gracelin.com**

New York City's current and former chancellors have praised **Torrey Maldonado** as a top teacher and author, and he has been recognized as a Top 10 Latino Author to Read and Watch. He has taught for over twenty years in his childhood hometown of Brooklyn. His middle-grade titles include *Tight*, which won a Christopher Award and was named a *Washington Post* and NPR Best Book of the Year, *What Lane?*, and *Secret Saturdays*. Growing up, Torrey hated books because "they were boring or seemed to hate or dismiss people where I'm from." Culturally responsive books and educators inspired him to teach and write. He was voted a Top Latino Author and best Middle Grade and Young Adult Novelist for African Americans, and his work reflects his and his students' experiences and is praised for its current feel, realness, and universal themes. torreymaldonado.com

 **Meg Medina** is the author of numerous award-winning works for children and teens. An advocate for Latinx readers and writers of every age, she examines how cultures intersect, as seen through the eyes of children. Her awards and recognitions include the 2019 Newbery Medal *(Merci Suárez Changes Gears)*, a Charlotte Huck Honor, a Pura Belpré Award and Honor, and the Ezra Jack Keats New Writer Award. She has also been a finalist for both the *Kirkus* Prize and the *Los Angeles Times* Book Prize and long-listed for the National Book Award. She lives with her family in Richmond, Virginia. megmedina.com

 **Christopher Myers** is a multimedia artist, an essayist, and a writer who is widely acclaimed for his work with literature for young people. Christopher is the creative director of Make Me a World, an imprint of Random House Children's Books committed to publishing stories for children that reflect our diverse world, and his projects include collaborations with artisans around the globe and mentorship

of a burgeoning new generation of creators. Christopher's writing and artwork has garnered him several awards, including a Caldecott Honor, several Coretta Scott King Honors, and a *Boston Globe-Horn Book* Honor. His celebrated picture book *My Pen* brings a sketchbook to life, and his forthcoming works include *We Have Wings*, the book version of the Joyce Award–winning play *Cartography* by Christopher and directed by Kaneza Schaal, and *Know What You Know: A Dialogue Between Father and Son*, a conversation with his father, Walter Dean Myers. Christopher lives in Brooklyn, New York. **kalyban.com**

 **Daniel Nayeri** is the publisher of Odd Dot, an imprint of Macmillan Children's Publishing Group, where he oversees a team of designers, editors, and inventors creating joyful books for curious minds. Daniel was born in Iran and spent several years as a refugee before immigrating to Oklahoma at age eight with his family. He is the author of several books for young readers, including the memoir *Everything Sad Is Untrue* and *Straw House, Wood House, Brick House, Blow: Four Novellas*. He is a former professional pastry chef, and if he's not writing or baking, he's likely playing German board games or riding English motorcycles. **danielnayeri.com**

 **Zeke Peña** makes comics and illustrations as an accessible way to remix history and explore complex issues. He was born in Las Cruces, New Mexico, and grew up in El Paso, Texas. He has a degree in art history from the University of Texas at Austin and is self-taught in drawing and painting. He received the 2020 Ezra Jack Keats and Pura Belpré Illustrator Honor Awards for his first children's book, *My Papi*

*Has a Motorcycle*, written by Isabel Quintero. He also received the 2018 *Boston Globe-Horn Book* Award for *Photographic: The Life of Graciela Iturbide*, a graphic biography he illustrated. He has published work with REMEZCLA, *Vice* (online), NPR's *Latino USA*, *The Believer* magazine, The Nib, Penguin Random House, Algonquin Books, Holt/Macmillan, and Cinco Puntos Press. Zeke is currently digging into his family history to uncover stories for future books. **zpvisual.com**

Creativity champion **Peter H. Reynolds** is the author and illustrator of *The Dot, Ish, The Word Collector,* and *Say Something!,* inspiring children and "grown-up children" with his messages about creativity, bravery, and courageous self-expression. Peter is also the illustrator of *I Am Yoga, I Am Peace, I Am Human, I Am Love,* and *The Water Princess* with Susan Verde, and the Judy Moody series by Megan McDonald. Peter and his twin brother, Paul, launched the Reynolds Center for Teaching, Learning, and Creativity, a nonprofit organization encouraging creativity and innovation in teaching and learning. **reynoldstlc.org**

**Erin K. Robinson** is a fashion designer and an illustrator who trained as a fine artist at Parsons School of Design and at the Corcoran School of the Arts and Design. She works in a variety of mediums, including pen and ink, acrylics, and digital art. Her editorial illustrations have appeared in *O, The Oprah Magazine;* the *Washington Post;* the *Boston Globe;* and *Essence.* She is also an illustrator of children's books, including *Brave. Black. First.: 50+ African American Women Who Changed the World.*

Erin's travels have taken her to Asia, Africa, Europe, and South America, but her most recent influence comes from Brooklyn, New York, where the diversity of women of the diaspora has inspired her design business, Brooklyndolly. Erin divides her time between Washington, D.C., and Brooklyn, New York. **brooklyndolly.com**

**Traci Sorell** writes fiction and nonfiction as well as poems for children. Traci's lyrical story in verse, *At the Mountain's Base*, illustrated by Weshoyot Alvitre, is an American Indian Youth Literature Honor book and celebrates the bonds of family and history-making women pilots. Her middle-grade novel, *Indian No More*, with the late Charlene Willing McManis, won the American Indian Youth Literature Award. It explores the impact of federal termination and relocation policies on an Umpqua family in the 1950s. Her debut nonfiction picture book, *We Are Grateful: Otsaliheliga*, illustrated by Frané Lessac, won a Robert F. Sibert Honor, a *Boston Globe-Horn Book* Honor, an American Indian Youth Literature Honor, and an NCTE Orbis Pictus Honor, along with four starred reviews. A former federal Indian law attorney and policy advocate, she is an enrolled citizen of the Cherokee Nation and lives in northeastern Oklahoma, where her tribe is located. **tracisorell.com**

**Shadra Strickland** is an illustrator whose works include *A Place Where Hurricanes Happen*, *Bird*, and *A Child's Book of Prayers and Blessings*. She has won an Ezra Jack Keats New Illustrator Award, a Coretta Scott King-John Steptoe Award for New Talent, and an NAACP Image Award. She is also a professor of illustration at the Maryland Institute College of Art. **jumpin.shadrastrickland.com**

**Don Tate** is an award-winning author and the illustrator of numerous critically acclaimed books for children. He is also one of the founding hosts of *The Brown Bookshelf*—a blog designed to push awareness of the myriad African American voices writing for young readers. Don frequently speaks at schools, public libraries, and writing conferences, and participates at book festivals around the country. Some of his illustrated titles include *Whoosh! Lonnie Johnson's Super-Soaking Stream of Inventions*, *The Amazing Age of John Roy Lynch*, and *Hope's Gift*. Additionally, he is the creator of *Poet: The Remarkable Story of George Moses Horton*, which won an Ezra Jack Keats New Writer Award, and the author of *It Jes' Happened: When Bill Traylor Started to Draw*, an Ezra Jack Keats New Writer Honor Book. Most recently, he has written *Strong as Sandow: How Eugen Sandow Became the Strongest Man on Earth*. **dontate.com**

**MaryBeth Timothy** is a Cherokee artist based in northeastern Oklahoma who loves creating images that speak to an audience. Adept in many mediums, she draws her inspiration from her love of nature and her heritage. MaryBeth has shown her award-winning art across the United States and in Europe. Her work has adorned a variety of magazine covers and is featured in publications such as *Indian Country Today*, *Green Country Living*, and *Oklahoma Magazine*. In 2019, Rogers State University TV highlighted MaryBeth in its Cherokee Artist Profile series. **moonhawkart.com**

**Duncan Tonatiuh** (toh-nah-tee-YOU) is both an author and an illustrator. His books have received multiple accolades, among them the Pura Belpré Medal, the Robert F. Sibert Medal, and a pair of

*New York Times* Best Illustrated Children's Book of the Year awards. Duncan is both Mexican and American. His illustrations are inspired by pre-Columbian art. His aim is to create images and stories that honor the past but are relevant to people, especially children, nowadays. **duncantonatiuh.com**

**Renée Watson** is a *New York Times* bestselling author. Her picture books and novels for teens have received several awards and international recognition, including her young adult novel *Piecing Me Together*, which received a Coretta Scott King Award and Newbery Honor. She has given readings and lectures at many renowned venues, including the United Nations, the Library of Congress, and the U.S. Embassy in Japan. Her poetry and fiction often center on the experiences of Black girls and women and explore themes of home, identity, and the intersections of race, class, and gender. **reneewatson.net**

**Valerie Wilson Wesley** has written numerous books for children, among them the Willimena Rules! series, *Freedom's Gifts: A Juneteenth Story*, and *AFRO-BETS Book of Black Heroes from A to Z*, which she cowrote with Wade Hudson. She is also the author of the Tamara Hayle mystery series for adults. Her novel *Ain't Nobody's Business If I Do* received the Black Caucus of the American Library Association's Literary Award. She also wrote two adult paranormal romances, *When the Night Whispers* and *The Moon Tells Secrets*, under the pen name Savanna Welles. Most of her mysteries and several of her novels have been published in Germany, France, and Great Britain. She is a former executive editor of *Essence* magazine. **valeriewilsonwesley.com**

 **Sharon Dennis Wyeth** has written over fifty books for children of all ages: picture books, middle grade, young adult, and across genres, including historical fiction and romance. Akin to the tradition of "family literature," Sharon's books are meant to be shared and discussed. Her stories grapple with difficult and complex issues, such as poverty, racism, and separation from family members, yet her writing is also characterized by optimism and hope. Her award-winning titles include *Something Beautiful, The Granddaughter Necklace, Once on This River, Always My Dad,* Corey's Underground Railroad Diaries and the Pen Pals series, and others. A graduate of Harvard University with an MFA from Hunter College, Sharon is a Cave Canem Poetry fellow and a visiting associate professor at Hollins University. **sharondenniswyeth.com**

# PHOTO CREDITS